Superior

Campfires

*A complete guide to successful
campfires including skits,
cheers, introductions, riddles
and Scouting legends*

Thomas Mercaldo

Printed in the United States
Eighth Printing

Aquinas Scout Books
C/O Thomas C. Mercaldo
154 Herbert Street
Milford, CT 06461
(203) 876-2822

Scout Fun Books is not officially affiliated with the Boy Scouts of
America, Girl Scouts of America, Scouts Canada or the World
Organization of Scouting.

BoyScoutBooks@aol.com

Scout Fun Books can be purchased on a wholesale basis for resale in
Camp Stores, Scout Shops and Trading Posts. For details write to us at
the above address or contact us by email at BoyScoutBooks@aol.com.

Preface

A successful campfire can be the highlight of any Scouting adventure. Campfires bring Scouts together and offer an opportunity for everyone to be an active participant in the fun.

How can you insure that your campfire is a success? *Superior Campfires* is a tool to help you get started. It contains examples of all the elements that can be a part of a successful campfire, including introductions, songs, stories, skits, riddles, jokes, cheers, one-liners, and Scouting legends. This guide can be used as an excellent starting point for new Scoutmasters, or as a source for new ideas for experienced leaders.

I sincerely hope that you enjoy *Superior Campfires*, and that it helps you create truly outstanding campfires.

Tom Mercaldo

Elements of a Successful Campfire

A successful campfire is usually fast paced and gets everyone involved. Humorous introductions, one-liners and cheers are a great way to keep things moving between performers. Audience participation stories and songs with repetition (echo songs) are another great way to get everyone involved. Skits can also be used effectively to get Scouts involved; some Scouts can perform skits, while others can be selected as "volunteers."

Non-toxic chemicals can be used to give your campfire color. When using these chemicals be sure to select materials that will not make smoke that is hazardous to breath. Opening and closing ceremonies can also add to the mystique of the event. Use the following checklist as a tickler to help you plan your campfire:

- ❏ Will you do something interesting to light the fire?
- ❏ Do you have an Opening Ceremony planned?
- ❏ One-liners or Run-ons? ❏ Scary Stories?
- ❏ Songs? ❏ Group Participation Stories?
- ❏ Humorous Stories? ❏ Do you have a closing planned?
- ❏ Skits?
- ❏ Cheers?
- ❏ Jokes/Riddles?

Table of Contents

Building and Lighting a Campfire

It is important that your campfire is built correctly, using dry dead wood and plenty of kindling. The worst way to begin a campfire is with a slow starting or non-burning pile of wood. There are many techniques for building a campfire; however the log cabin style approach is generally best if the campfire is targeted for a large audience. The Log-Cabin fire consists of a crisscross lay fire made with large logs, with smaller crisscross lays piled in rows on top. A long burning fire can be created by lighting the upper fire lay and letting the fire eat its way to the bottom. Complete instructions on fire building can be found in many publications, including the Boy Scout Handbook™.

You can add flare to your campfire by using creative methods to ignite the wood. **The Candle Method** is one such approach. Secure a candle to a block of wood, with clear fishing line attached to the wood block. Take a metal coffee can and cut out one third of the cylinder. Place the coffee can bottom up in the fireplace, then place the candle on the wood block under the coffee can. When it is time to start the fire secretly pull on the end of the fishing line and the fire will appear to start magically.

Another interesting approach to starting a campfire is to have an older Scout or adult leader dress as an Indian. This Scouter can play the part of a generic Indian or can be dressed as Akela or Chief Sequassen. At the proper time, the **Indian Runner** can sprint in with a torch to light the campfire. Or, if your campfire is held near a lake, the Indian can approach the fire circle in a canoe. If you wish to incorporate several Scouts into an opening ceremony to light a campfire, the following ceremony which requires four Scouts can be used:

The North Wind brings the cold that brings endurance,
A torch bearer enters the fire circle from the north.
The South Wind brings the warmth of friendship,
A torch bearer enters the fire circle from the south.
The East Wind brings the light of day,
A torch bearer enters the fire circle from the east.
The West Wind, from the direction where the sun sinks, brings night and stars.
A torch bearer enters the fire circle from the west.
On direction from the MC, all light the fire.

Many other opening ceremonies are available (including the ash ceremony found on the next page) or could be developed to make your campfire special.

A third popular approach to lighting a campfire is known as the **Magic Fireball**. With this method a ball of fire will appear to descend from the sky to the heart of the fire lay, immediately igniting the fire. You will need a wooden spool, fishing line, and some type of metal wire to make the magic fireball work. String the wooden spool onto the fishing line and attach the line securely to the fire lay and to a tree. Attach bandage gauze or some other flammable material to the spool to serve as the fireball. A Scout concealed in the tree can then light the fireball and send it down the string into the fireplace. Be sure to practice this several times before the campfire; the angle of the string, the weight of the spool and the flammable material used can all impact whether or not the magic fireball will work properly.

Liquid and gas fuels should not be used in fire starting ceremonies at Scouting events. Model rocket igniters or match friction igniters are not generally prohibited but should only be used with caution by individuals knowledgeable in such fire starting techniques.

During the lighting process, chants can be said, or songs can be sung to encourage the fire to start. These chants are short groups of words repeated slowly at first and faster as the fire starts. One such chant is "Burn Fire Burn, Burn Fire Burn, etc."

If you decide to sing songs during the fire lighting, it is important to select songs that can be learned quickly or that nearly everyone already knows. It is important to get everyone participating from the start so popular patriotic songs or songs featuring repetition are good choices. Other songs like Birds in the Wilderness or Boom Chick a Boom make good icebreakers at campfires.

The Campfire Ash Ceremony (Ashes of Friendship)

The taking of ashes from one campfire to another is a ceremony done by Boy Scouts all around the world. The main purpose of these ashes is to help Scouts recognize the international aspect of the world brotherhood of scouting. Ashes taken from a campfire are sprinkled into the flames of the next campfire. The day after a campfire when the ashes are cold, they are stirred and each Scout present at the ceremony takes some ashes to mix in with the next campfire. Each Scout keeps a list of all of the campfires that they have sprinkled their ashes in. If more than one Scout brings ashes to the campfire, the lists are combined and the dates and places of all campfires are recorded and passed on. As Boy Scouts travel, the ashes circle the globe. It is a tradition that only those actually present at the campfire can receive ashes from the ceremony to carry on to another campfire.

The Ceremony

We carry our friendships with us in these ashes from other campfires with comrades in other lands. May the joining of the past fires with the leaping flames of this campfire symbolize once more the unbroken chain that binds scouts of all nations together.

With greetings from our brothers around the world, I will add these ashes and the fellowship therein, to our campfire. Will anyone with campfire ashes please come forward and join me.

Wait for others to come forward with ashes.

The ashes I spread into this campfire carry memories of past campfires dating back to _____

I will now add these ashes to the campfire.

So that you may pass these ashes on and share them with others at your next campfire, you will be given a history of where these ashes have been. *Recite history of ashes added to fire.*

One-Liners (aka Run-Ons or Walk-Ons)

Successful campfires tend to be fast paced; one-liners are a great way to avoid any breaks in the action. Immediately following any song or skit, one-liners can be acted out to allow for transition to the next event. Examples of some good one-liners follow:

Be Prepared

There are several variations of the "Be Prepared" Skit, here are the most popular.

A Scout walks to the middle of the crowd, stands at attention, salutes, and yells "BE PREPARED." This action is repeated by two other Scouts. When they are all standing side by side, some surprise action is precipitated from behind the audience. Possible surprise actions might include: loud sounds, (like the sound of a motorized horn or a bullhorn) water, (spray the crowd from behind on a warm night), water balloons, leaves, (drop a large volume of leaves from above the audience), etc.

An alternative approach is for a different Scout to come out between each skit and say "BE PREPARED." The surprise activity then follows the third Scout.

The Briefcase

A Scout walks on stage holding a briefcase. The MC asks him what he is doing. The Scout responds, "I'm taking my case to court."

The same Scout enters the stage following another skit. Again he is carrying a briefcase and optionally, he can carry a small step ladder. The MC again asks him what he is doing. The Scout responds, "I'm taking my case to a higher court."

The Scout again walks on stage holding a briefcase. The MC asks him what he is doing. The Scout asks the MC to stretch out his arm. The MC complies. The Scout places the briefcase in the MC's arms and responds, "I'm resting my case."

The MC discards the case and introduces another song. After the song the Scout walks back on stage looking all around. The MC again asks him what he is doing. The Scout responds, "I've lost my case."

Parental Warning

The Master of Ceremonies randomly calls on a Scoutmaster and asks, "Did your parents ever tell you that if you made weird facial expressions, your face might freeze like that?" When the Scoutmaster says, "Yes", the MC replies, "Well, you can't say you were never warned."

Coffee

The Scoutmaster approaches a Scout complaining, "This coffee tastes like mud."
The Scout responds, "That's funny, it was just ground this morning."

Boy Dragging Rope

A Scout is seen dragging a rope around the stage area. The master of ceremonies asks, "Why are you dragging that rope?" The Scout responds, "It beats pushing it."

Good for Nothing

This one-liner requires a Scout, and a Scoutmaster who doesn't take himself too seriously. The Scout walks up to the Scout leader and says, "If I'm good throughout the entire camping trip will you give me $10.00?" The Scout leader responds, "When I was your age, I was good for nothing."

Painting the Walls

A Scout walks in holding a paint brush and bucket. He is wearing two winter coats. He interrupts the MC stating that he is a painter, and he needs to paint this area. The MC asks him why he is dressed for winter. The painter responds that he was told to paint the area with two coats.

Spot Announcement

MC: I have just been handed a note that we need to interrupt our program for a Spot announcement.

Scout: (*offstage*) Woof, Woof.

MC: Thank you Spot.

Smoke Signals

Scout 1: Look over there, smoke signals. I wonder what they say.

Scout 2: I can read smoke signals. The message says..... HELP.....MY ........SLEEPING......BAG..... IS....ON.....FIRE.

Important News Flash

As scout comes forward and says, "We interrupt this program for an important news flash." This statement is followed by the Scout, turning on and off a flashlight that is pointed at the audience.

Wire for the Scoutmaster

A Scout runs on stage yelling, "Wire for the Scoutmaster, I have a wire for the Scoutmaster."
The Scoutmaster responds, "I'm the Scoutmaster."
Then the Scout hands him a wire.

The Infantry is Coming

A Scout runs on stage yelling, "The infantry is coming, the infantry is coming!" Later (you can do this a few seconds later or after the next song or skit), a second Scout comes out yelling "The infantry is coming! The infantry is coming!" This happens three or four times. Finally, one or two Scouts come out holding a small tree and they proclaim, "The infant tree is here!"

They're After Me

A Scout runs on stage yelling, "They're after me, they're after me."
The MC replies, "Who's after you."
The Scout answers, "The Squirrels, they think I'm nuts."

Throwing Up

A Scout walks across the stage tossing a ball in the air.
The MC asks, "What are you doing?"
The Scout replies, "I'm throwing up!"

The jokes in the Scout vs. Scoutmaster Section also make effective one-liners.

Skits

Skits are generally the corner stone of a successful campfire. Skits that are humorous fast paced and involve the audience generally work best. Here are a few sample skits that are generally effective:

The Four Seasons

The narrator begins by asking four volunteers to participate. Each volunteer is assigned a role in the skit; roles include a tree, a bird, a babbling brook, and the tree's lifeblood, the sap. Generally two of the volunteers are "plants" who know in advance their roles as the tree and the bird. The brook and the sap are then left to follow the careful instruction of the narrator. Each of the participants acts out their assigned role. For example, the tree raises his arms signifying leaves growing in the spring. He lowers his arms in the fall.

Narrator: To the babbling brook - you need to babble.

Brook: Babble, babble, babble....

Narrator: In the Spring, the leaves come out on the trees (the tree raises his arms above his head), the birds begin to sing (bird - chirp, chirp, chirp), and the brook begins to babble rapidly (brook starts babbling faster), and the sap, which provides valuable nutrients to the tree, begins to run (sap starts running).

The narrator continues to describe activities throughout summer and fall, and throughout this narration, the sap's job is to continue running at various paces. In the winter the dialog ends with a narration that goes something like this: In the winter the brook freezes and stops babbling (babbling stops). The birds are gone and the trees seem lifeless and without motion. But through it all there is still some activity, for you see, the sap keeps running.

Gathering of the Nuts

For this skit, the MC announces that the "Squirrel Patrol" will be performing the next skit. Members from the patrol walk around the crowd and select volunteers to help them with their skit. The volunteers are brought to the front of the campfire and members of the "Squirrel Patrol" sit down. The MC comes out and says let's give the Squirrel Patrol a big hand for that last skit which they like to call, "The Gathering of the Nuts."

The Fortune Teller

MC: I'd now like to introduce the amazing Felix who can tell you your fortune simply by smelling your shoe.

Felix: Thank you, thank you. Who would like to be my first volunteer? *(Felix selects a "plant" from the audience, the Scout comes forward takes off his shoe and hands it to Felix. Felix smells the shoe and predicts that a Scoutleader will give him a dollar. A nearby Scoutleader walks over and hands him a dollar.)*

Scout 1: Wow! Thanks a lot.

Felix: Who will be my next volunteer? *(Felix selects a "plant" from the audience, the Scout comes forward takes off his shoe and hands it to Felix. Felix smells the shoe and predicts that a Scoutleader will give him two dollars. A nearby Scoutleader walks over and hands him two dollars).*

Scout 2: Wow! Thanks a lot.

Felix: Who will be my next volunteer? *(This time Felix selects an unsuspecting victim. The victim takes off his shoe and hands it to Felix. Felix throws the shoe to the back of the audience and says)* I predict you will go for a long walk.

The Lawn Mower

This skit requires two Scouts, one serves as the announcer, the other acts like a lawn mower. The first Scout pretends to pull the string in order to start the mower. The mower sputters but refuses to start. The first Scout then calls for volunteers to try and start the mower. The final volunteer successfully starts the mower, and the first Scout explains that all it took to start the mower was a big jerk.

Suckers on the Line

Two people walk on stage with a long rope stretched between them. One of the Scouts explains that he is a fisherman, the other explains that he runs the local fish market. They attempt to contact each other by phone, and the fisherman acts as if he can't hear the fish market manager. Volunteers are brought forward to hold up the line. When several volunteers are up holding the rope, the fisherman and the fish market manager can finally hear each other. The fisherman says that he doesn't have any salmon, but he did catch a bunch of suckers on the line.

14

J. C. Penney

Scout 1 is standing in the middle of the stage as several other Scouts walk by one at a time.

(A Scout walks by wearing jeans)
Scout 1: Hey, where did you get those great jeans?
Scout 2: J. C. Penney.
(A Scout walks by wearing a jacket)
Scout 1: Where'd you get that great jacket?
Scout 3: J. C. Penney.
(A Scout walks by wearing sneakers)
Scout 1: Where'd you get those cool sneakers?
Scout 4: J. C. Penney.
(A Scout walks by wearing nothing but a towel)
Scout 1: Who are you?
Scout 5: J. C. Penney.

This skit can also be done as L. L. Bean or Montgomery Ward.

Slow Motion Theft

Two pickpockets announce to the crowd that they will demonstrate their incredible skill at their profession. The pickpockets begin walking toward an oncoming pedestrian. They quickly brush up against the pedestrian and continue on their way. When the pedestrian disappears, they show all the things they stole from him *(use whatever is handy like a wallet, comb, or jackknife, be sure to show a lot of stuff)*.

The pickpockets then ask the audience if they would like to see in slow motion, how the theft was done. They return the stuff to the pedestrian *(make sure the pedestrian puts the stuff in pockets where it will fall out easily)* and re-enact the routine walking super slow. The pickpockets bump into the pedestrian, pick him up, turn him upside down and shake him vigorously until all the stuff falls out. The pickpockets drop him on the ground, pick up the stuff, put it in their pockets, pick up the pedestrian, set him back on his feet and all parties continue on their way.

Crossing the Delaware

If a rowboat from camp is available, it makes this skit work much more effectively. A group of Scouts are sitting in a rowboat. One Scout stands in the front. The MC introduces this group as George Washington and his men crossing the Delaware. The MC gives this situation a big buildup, describing how tired the troops must be and suggests that everyone listen to George Washington's inspirational direction as they reach shore.

When the MC is finished speaking a Scout yells, "Hooray we've reached shore." George Washington says, "OK everybody, get out of the boat."

Igor

A mad scientist has created a monster named Igor. With pride, the scientist talks about how he can conquer the world with the help of Igor whom he has taught to obey three different commands. Scouts come to the mad scientist's door under different pretenses, to sell magazines, Girl Scout cookies, Mary Kay cosmetics, etc., and each time the mad scientist disposes of them by using the following series of commands:

Igor Stand: Igor stands slowly.
Igor Walk: Igor stiffly walks.
Igor Kill: Igor strangles the salesperson.

After killing each victim, Igor goes back to his place and lies down.
The Skit ends with the mad scientist going to the front of the stage wringing his hands. *(He can no longer see Igor).* I can conquer the world, he says, with just three simple commands:

Igor Stand: Igor stands slowly.
Igor Walk: Igor stiffly walks.
Igor Kill: Igor strangles the mad scientist.

Rough Riders

Two Scouts are lying in sleeping bags; one is in a tent, the other just outside it. A group of bikers come by and say, "Hey, let's beat up on this guy in the sleeping bag." After this happens, the Scout that was beaten wakes up his friend and tells him what happened. His friend tells him it was just a dream and to go back to sleep. The bikers come back and again beat on the Scout sleeping outside. After they leave he arouses his friend who again tells him it was just a dream. However to make him feel safer they agree to change places. The bikers come back a third time and the skit ends with one of the bikers saying, "This guy's had enough, let's get the guy in the tent this time."

The Restaurant

This skit requires at least two scouts and some volunteers

The narrator initiates this skit by asking for a volunteer. This volunteer is instructed to get on his hands and knees to serve as a bar or table. Next, additional volunteers are instructed to sit next to the table and they are told to converse while the waiter offers them a drink. The waiter then places two water glasses on the table (the back of the first volunteer), while the customers are chatting. The skit ends when the customers are told the restaurant is closed and it is time to leave. The "table" is left with the job of trying to get up without spilling water on his back.

Cheers

Cheers are a good way to insure the participation of everyone in attendance at a campfire. Some cheers are humorous, some can be done in a round, and others may require a level of skill or group co-ordination. Cheers are mostly, however, a good way to acknowledge the contributions of performers in a song or skit.

Hat in the Air Cheer

With this cheer, a leader throws their hat in the air. Scouts try to make as much noise as possible while the hat is in the air. When the hat hits the ground, all noise stops.

Bottle Cheer

One hand is clenched in a slightly hollow fist and is struck with the palm of the other hand against the thumb and forefinger. This motion is similar to trying to get ketchup out of a bottle.

We Will Rock You

To the tune of a well-known song have everyone repeat, "We will, we will, - rock you!" more emphasis should be placed on the words "rock you." This cheer is usually done to a rhythmic clap that consists of two foot stomps followed by a single hand clap as follows:

Stomp, Stomp, Clap - Stomp, Stomp, Clap - Stomp, Stomp, Clap.

Campbell's Soup Cheer

In unison, Scouts say, "Mmmmm, Mmmm, Good."

Cookie Cheer

The leader announces that the last skit deserves the cookie cheer. Each Scout places their right hand above their head as if they are holding a cookie. In unison, they pretend to crush the cookie in their hand and say, "crummy, crummy, crummy."

Fortune Cookie Cheer

Similar to the cookie cheer but substitute "Fooey, Fooey, Fooey" for "crummy, crummy, crummy."

Big Round of Applause

Scouts hold both their hands together above their heads. A "cheer" leader says, "Let's give that last performer a round of applause;" the leader then makes a big circle with his hands, bringing them back together by his feet with a single clap. This is a round applause.

Orchestrated Applause

A group leader places his hands out like a symphony director and applause begins. If he lowers his hands Scouts should clap slower and softly. By raising his hands above his heads applause should become louder and faster.

The Symphony Director

A leader divides the group into multiple sections and tells each group to play the part of an instrument. One group can clap in unison like a base drum, another group can be the tuba section verbally repeating "omm pa, omm pa." Additional instruments can be added, and Scouts can whistle, hum, or bop (open their mouths and hit them with a hand) to represent these other sections. The leader then points to a group and asks them to perform. By pointing up the group should perform loudly, pointing down should lower the volume of the team.

"Reverse" applause

Scouts hold their hands apart as if to applaud. Instead of clapping however, Scouts move their hands apart making no sound.

The Clam Cheer

Each Scout is instructed to hold one hand above their heads. They begin making a sound by bringing the fingers of the raised hand down into the palm. This motion is like that of a clam opening and closing its shell. The slight sound is similar to applause, but is a little less than deafening.

The Flintstone Cheer

Each Scout is instructed to shake their hands over their heads while yelling, "Yabba-dabba-do."

Pow Wow Cheer

Divide the audience into two groups. The first is instructed to say, "POW," the second "WOW." Each group yells out their assigned word when the Leader points to them.

Ugie-Aye

Leader: ugie ugie ugie
Scouts: aye, aye, aye
Leader: ugie, ugie, ugie
Scouts: aye, aye, aye
Leader: ugie
Scouts: aye
Leader: ugie
Scouts: aye
Leader: ugie ugie ugie
Scouts: aye, aye, aye

This cheer can also be done as "Echo, echo, echo," where the word "echo" is used in place of the word "ugie."

Pinky Cheer

Scouts clap their pinky fingers together making almost no sound.

Chinese Bow Cheer

Scouts stand up, fold their arms and face the performers. Then in unison they bow at the waist and say, "Ah phooey."

Great Job Cheer

With this cheer the audience is broken into two groups. The first group is instructed to say "Great" when the MC points to them. The second group is similarly instructed to say "Job." The MC points alternatively to each group on an accelerating basis.

Scallop Cheer

Scouts fold one arm over the other by placing the left hand on the right shoulder and by placing the right hand above the left onto the right shoulder. Then lift the right elbow up and down making a sound like a scallop opening and closing its shell.

Class A, B, & C

The Class A, B & C cheers are a series of claps repeated rapidly and in unison to the following cadence:

(1-2-3-4) (1-2) (1-2)
(1-2-3-4) (1-2) (1-2)
(1-2-3-4) (1-2-3-4) (Pause) (1)

The Class B Cheer is a variation where the last clap is omitted. Scouts who inadvertently include the final clap are called "Rookies."

(1-2-3-4) (1-2) (1-2)
(1-2-3-4) (1-2) (1-2)
(1-2-3-4) (1-2-3-4) (Pause)

The Class C Cheer features a longer pause before the final clap. Scouts should bring their hands toward each other as if to make the final clap but not make contact. Then they should try again this time making the final clap in unison.

(1-2-3-4) (1-2) (1-2)
(1-2-3-4) (1-2) (1-2)
(1-2-3-4) (1-2-3-4) (Pause) (Pause) (1)

Abe Lincoln Cheer

The audience is directed to say: That was great: Honest

Other Cheers - Triplets

For the following cheers the group leader gets Scouts to say the following word or phrases three times in unison:

Oil Well Cheer: Crude, crude, crude
Jolly Green Giant Cheer: Ho, ho, ho
Frankfurter Cheer: Hot dog, hot dog, hot dog
Lumberjack Cheer: Chop, chop, chop (tiimmbbeerrrr)
Ghost Cheer: Boo, boo, boo
Sad Ghost: Boo hoo, boo hoo, boo hoo
Indian: How, how, how
Cheese Cheer: Grate, grate, grate.
Squirrel Cheer: Nuts, nuts, nuts.

Scout Riddles

Sharing riddles and jokes can be a lot of fun, especially at small troop campfires.

Scout Lore

What should you do if you swallow a flashlight?
>   *Spit it out and be delighted.*

How many Scouts can you fit in an empty dining hall?
>   *One, then it is no longer empty.*

What do you get when you cross a monster and a Boy Scout?
>   *A creature that scares old ladies across the street.*

Why did the Scoutmaster put wheels on his rocking chair?
>   *He wanted to rock and roll.*

Why shouldn't you place a Scout camp near a chicken farm?
>   *You wouldn't want the campers to hear any fowl language.*

What made the skating Boy Scout dizzy?
>   *Too many good turns.*

Why did the Scoutleader plan a parade for 03/04/2050?
>   *He wanted the troops to march forth in the future.*

What happened to the Scout who put a firecracker in the pancake batter?
>   *When the pancakes came, he blew his stack.*

What happened to the Scout who ironed a four leaf clover?
>   *He really pressed his luck.*

What happened to the Scout who wanted to be a piece of firewood?
>   *He made a fuel of himself.*

Where will campers sleep in the 25th century?
>   *In the future tents.*

Why did the Scout stuff dollar bills in his shoe?
>   *He wanted to have a legal tender foot.*

What badge do you earn for greeting royalty?
>   *Hi King.*

The Wild Adirondack Cow

For those who do not live in the Northeast, this section requires a special introduction. The Wild Adirondack Cow is a carnivorous moose-like creature that inhabited the Adirondack and Berkshire valleys. Similar to a Holstein in shape and color, the much larger Wild Adirondack Cow features a wide jaw and bear-like teeth. Most scientists believe the Wild Adirondack Cow (WAC) is now extinct, nonetheless, many campers claim to have seen the creature in recent times. Tales about this vicious relative of the grizzly bear are a central theme in Indian folklore.

How do you keep a Wild Adirondack Cow from charging?
Take away his credit card

Why did the Wild Adirondack Cow say "Baa-baa, oink-oink?"
He was trying to learn a foreign language.

Where did the Wild Adirondack Cow go when he lost his tail?
To a retail store.

What do you call Wild Adirondack Cows that ride on trains?
Passengers.

What happened when the Wild Adirondack Cows entered the campground?
There was udder chaos.

What is black and white and blue all over?
A Wild Adirondack Cow at the north pole.

What is black and white and blue and hides in caves?
A Wild Adirondack Cow that's afraid of polar bears.

Where does a Wild Adirondack Cow go for entertainment?
To the mooovies

When should Wild Adirondack Cows blow their horns?
When they're stuck in traffic.

What did the Wild Adirondack Cow say after eating a DVD?
I liked the book better.

What do you call a Wild Adirondack Cow with no ears?
Whatever you want; he can't hear you.

The Animals at Camp

What does Smokey the Bear put in his backpack before a long hike?
Simply the bear essentials

Why aren't the elephants at camp allowed on the beach?
Because they can't keep their trunks up.

What do you call a hundred rabbits walking backwards?
A receding hare line.

What has a yellow stomach and sucks sap from trees?
A yellow bellied sap sucker.

If camp animals played baseball, which one would be the best hitter?
A Bat.

How come only small toads can sit under toadstools?
Because there isn't mushroom.

Can skunks have babies?
No they can only have skunks.

What does a skunk do when it gets mad?
It raises a stink.

What is the last hair on a skunk's tail called?
A skunk hair.

What animals can jump higher than the tallest trees at camp?
All animals. Trees can't jump.

Why did the crow look for a telephone?
He wanted to make a long distance caw.

What is black and white and goes around and around?
A skunk in a revolving door.

In an outdoor Chapel, where does a skunk sit?
In a pew.

How do you stop a mouse from squeaking?
With a little motor oil.

Why was the mother owl worried about her son?
Because he didn't give a hoot about anything.

Joe Boy Scout

Why did Joe Scout take a ruler to bed?
He wanted to see how long he would sleep.

Why did Joe Scout reach for a bar of soap when his canoe overturned?
He thought he would wash up on shore.

Why did Joe Scout tie a flashlight to his bed?
Because he was a light sleeper.

What happened when Joe Scout swallowed some uranium?
He got atomic ache.

Why did Joe Scout buy a set of tools?
Because everyone kept telling him he had a screw loose.

Why did Joe Scout tiptoe past his tent?
He didn't want to wake up the sleeping bags.

Why did Joe Scout buy a package of bird seed?
He wanted to grow birds in his garden.

Why was Joe Scout glad he wasn't an Eagle?
He couldn't fly.

Why did Joe Scout eat a light bulb?
He was in need of a little light refreshment.

Why did Joe Scout stare at the orange juice container?
It said concentrate on it.

Why did Joe Scout put an ice-pack in his father's sleeping bag?
He wanted to have a cold pop.

Why did Joe Scout sell his alarm clock?
It kept going off when he was asleep.

Why did Joe Scout pour pancake batter on his electric blanket?
He wanted breakfast in bed.

Why did Joe Scout spray bug spray on his watch?
He wanted to get rid of the ticks.

Why did Joe Scout act like a nut?
He wanted to catch a squirrel.

Scout versus Scoutmaster

Scoutmaster: Each of you needs to eat all of your vegetables. There are thousands of starving children who would love to have them.
Scout: Name two.

Scoutmaster: Why do you always have to answer my questions with another question?
Scout: Why not?

Scout: If I'm good throughout the entire camping trip will you give me a dollar?
Scoutmaster: Absolutely not! When I was your age I was good for nothing.

Scout: I'm too tired to wash the dishes.
Scoutmaster: Nonsense, a little hard work never killed anyone.
Scout: Then why should I run the risk of being the first?

Scoutmaster: Why are you guys returning so late from the orienteering course?
Scout: We were following this Tates compass, but it kept sending us in circles.
Scoutmaster: You idiots. Don't you know he who has a Tates is lost!

Scoutmaster: Your short story entitled, "My Dog," reads exactly the same as your brothers.
Scout: It's the same dog sir.

Scout: My tent mate thinks he's a refrigerator.
Scoutmaster: Don't let it bother you.
Scout: I can't help it. He's sleeping with his mouth open, and the light is keeping me awake.

Scout: I can't sleep.
Scoutmaster: Lie down in the fireplace; you'll sleep like a log.

Scout Jokes

Scout Stories

The Scoutmaster decided to try to use some psychology to try to get his lazy Scouts to do some work. So he said, "I've got a nice easy job for the laziest Scout here. Any volunteers?"

In an instant all but one of the Scouts raised their hands. "Why didn't you raise your hand?" the Scoutmaster asked him.
"Too much work," he replied.

The highlight of the Troop 19 annual winter campout was the ice fishing competition. Each patrol drilled holes in the ice and began fishing. After several minutes the Eagle patrol was reeling in one fish after another, while the other patrols continued to have no luck. A young Scout approached the Eagle patrol leader and asked what he was doing wrong.

"Ymm umm wmm umm," the Patrol Leader replied.
"What?" asked the boy again.
"Ymm umm wmm umm," he said again.
"What?"
Finally, the patrol leader spit a bunch of worms into his hand and said, "You have to keep the worms warm."

Two Scouts were walking through the woods when suddenly a mountain lion leaped out in front of them. The first Scout cautioned the second to remain calm. "Remember what we read in the Scout Handbook. If you stand absolutely still and look the lion straight in the eye, he will turn and run away."

The second Scout said, "Fine, you've read the Scout handbook, and I've read the handbook, but has the lion read the handbook?"

Once there was a boy whose parents named him Odd. Throughout his life, everyone teased him about his name. As he grew old, he wrote out his final wishes. "I've been the butt of jokes all my life," he said. "I don't want people making fun of me after I'm gone." He asked to be buried in the middle of the wilderness with a tombstone that does not bear his name.

After his death, people stumbled upon the large blank stone and said, "That's odd."

After annoying patrol members with difficult first aid questions, and yelling when questions were answered wrong, the senior patrol leader turned the meeting over to the ASPL. The ASPL reviewed first aid with the troop at great length. After completing a lengthy discussion on tourniquets, the ASPL asked, "What would you do if the Senior Patrol Leader received a serious head wound?"

Without hesitation patrol members responded in unison, "Put a tourniquet around his neck."

A young Scout was interested in earning the first aid merit badge. As part of the test, the Scoutmaster asked what items should be included in a first aid kit. The Scout listed many items including a jar of mayonnaise.

"Why would you put a jar of mayonnaise in a first aid kit?" the Scoutmaster inquired.

"Because," the young Scout replied, "it says in the Scout Handbook to 'include a dressing.' "

A Scoutmaster stopped in to see his Psychiatrist. "Doc you've got to help me. I keep having the same dream over and over again, and I can't get rid of it."

"Tell me about your dream," the psychiatrist stated.

The Scoutmaster responded, "The first night I dreamt about wigwams. The next night I dreamt about teepees. Then wigwams. Then teepees, then...."

"Wait a minute," the psychiatrist interrupted. "I think I know what your problem is. You're just two tents."

Two Scouts were walking through the woods when suddenly, they stumbled upon a large black bear. Immediately, one of the two removed his hiking books, reached into his pack, and slipped on a pair of running shoes. "What are you doing," his companion asked incredulously. "You know that you can't outrun a bear, even with those on."

"Who cares about the bear," the first hiker replied. "All I need to worry about is outrunning you."

Did you hear about the Scoutmaster who threatened to kill his Scouts if they didn't collect the morning mist in a bottle? It was a case of dew or die.

Joe Scout

Joe Scout was telling his fellow Scouts how getting the first aid merit badge had prepared him for an emergency. "I saw a women hit by a truck," he stated, "She had a twisted ankle, broken bones and a fractured skull."

"How terrible! What did you do?"

"Thanks to my first-aid training, I knew just how to handle it. I sat on the ground and put my head between my knees to keep from fainting."

Joe Scout decided to take up painting so he went to the store to buy an easel. At the art supply store they carried two sizes small and large. Joe thought about it for a while and decided to choose the lesser of two easels.

Joe Scout was trying to light a match. He struck one, but it wouldn't light. He struck a second, but it didn't burn either. Finally, he struck the third match and it lit right up. "That's a good one!" Joe proclaimed as he blew out the match. "I'll have to save it."

Joe Scout got careless with matches and lit the field behind his house on fire. Thinking quickly he ran into the house and called the fire department.

"The field is on fire!" Joe Scout cried into the phone.

"Calm down," the dispatcher intoned. "Now how do we get to the field?"

"Don't you still have that red truck?" Joe inquired.

A women lion tamer had the vicious animals under such complete control that she could command them to take a lump of sugar from her lips and they would obey. Joe Scout stood skeptically by the cage and yelled, "Anyone could do that."

The ringmaster came over and asked, "Would you like to try?"

"Sure," replied Joe Scout. "But first get those crazy lions out of there!"

Joe Scout ordered a large pizza. The cook pulled the pizza out of the oven and asked Joe Scout, "Do you want me to cut it into 6 or 8 pieces?"

"Better make it six," Joe Scout responded, "I could never eat eight pieces."

Joe Scout visited Toronto with plans to try his hand at ice fishing. He pitched his tent and got ready to cut a hole in the ice. As he pulled the cord on his chain saw, he heard a voice from above, "There are no fish under the ice."

He pulled the cord again, and the same voice emanated from above, "There are no fish under the ice."

Awestruck, Joe Scout looked reverently at the heavens. "Is that you God," he inquired.

"No," the voice replied. "I own this rink, and I can tell you, there are no fish under the ice."

When Joe Scout first went to camp, a group of boys convinced him to try his hand at elephant hunting. Several hours after he started, he returned to camp empty handed.

"You didn't catch anything, did ya," one of the boys asked Joe Scout.

"No, I gave up because the decoys got too heavy," Joe Scout replied.

Joe Scout handed his teacher a drawing featuring an airplane covered with grapes, apples, bananas and oranges. Puzzled, the teacher turned to Joe and said, "Today's drawings were supposed to be related to patriotic American songs. How is that drawing related to our topic?"

"You know the song America the Beautiful," Joe Scout replied. "Well that's the fruited plane."

Joe Scout and the members of Troop 00, visited a farm for the first time. "I've been watching that bull over there for some time," Joe Scout related, "and I don't understand how come he doesn't have any horns."

"Well," replied the farmer, "sometimes we saw off the horns when they're young so the bulls don't poke us. The horns sometimes fall off the older bulls. As for that bull there, the reason why he doesn't have any horns is because he's a horse."

After breaking his arm, Joe Scout asked the doctor, "Will I be able to play the violin when the cast comes off?"

"Of course you will," replied the doctor.

"That's great," stammered Joe. "I always wished I could play the violin."

Joe Scout's Famous Quotes

These humorous quotes can be used by the MC as a way to keep the audience entertained between skits:

You can't go out there cold turkey with egg on your face.

You can lead a horse to water - but you can't make him put on a swimsuit.

A horse may go to water, but a pencil must be lead.

You can lead a gift horse to water, but you can't look in his mouth.

Don't count you chickens before they cross the road.

He sank to new heights.

Beauty is only skin deep in the eye of the beholder.

Mind your own business before pleasure.

He's still green behind the ears.

He hitched his wagon to a car.

Seven days without food makes one weak.

A home where the buffalo roam is generally a very messy house.

He who laughs first shall be last.

Don't shoot until you see the whites of the egg on their face.

If at first you spill your milk, cry, cry again.

Two wrongs don't make a right, but three lefts do.

Never play hide and seek with a Peking duck.

Scout Definitions

Lemonade: Helping an old lemon across the street.
Hatchet: What a hen does to an egg.
Klondike derby: Winter hat.
Intense: Where people stay when they go camping.
Hermit: A girl's baseball glove.
Missing: To sing incorrectly.
Cold War: Snowball fight.
Indistinct: Place where Scouts wash dirty dishes.
Itch hiking: Hiking through poison ivy.
Canteen: Thirst aid kit.
Dandelion: Pretty nice fibbing.
Mushroom: Place where they serve meals at Scout camp.
Axe: Chopsticks.
Scholarship: A boat filled with very bright people.
Sea Scout: Scout that immediately follows the A and B Scouts.
    Or just another buoy Scout.
    Or Scouts that are not invisible.
Retired: What you get when you lose your second wind.
Bassinet: What Scouts hope for when fishing.
Monolog: A single piece of firewood.
Transparent: Mother or father of the invisible Boy Scout.
Income tax: Capital punishment.
Shamrock: A bogus rock.
First aid kit: A cat that has medical training.
Illegal: A sick Scout who has earned the organizations highest rank.
    A sick bird.
Explain: An aircraft that no longer flies.
Coincide: What you should do if it starts raining.
Antipasto: Someone opposed to Italian cooking.
Research: When you search for something twice.
Information: How Air Force planes fly.
Raincoat: Thunderwear.
Trifle: A rifle with three barrels.
Hot chocolate: Stolen candy.
Flashlight: A case in which you carry dead batteries.
Impostor: Imitation spaghetti.
Boycott: A bed for a small male child.

Ice cream: What I do if someone hits me.

Acquire: A group of singers.

Compatible: An invitation to come pet a male cow.

Deduce: De lowest card in de deck.

Ideal: My turn to shuffle the cards.

Tenderfoot: What one gets if they drop a hammer on their foot.

Doctor: Second aid.

Alternate: What every Cub Scout does after they turn seven.

Tripidation: Fear of falling down.

Balanced Diet: A cookie in each hand.

Tater Tots: Children of couch potatoes.

Pillow: A nap sack.

Pronoun: A noun that has lost its amateur status.

Aftermath: The period following algebra.

Amino acid: Opposite of a nice old acid.

Will: Dead giveaway.

Haley's comment: I regret that I have only one life to give for my country.

Paradox: More than one but less than three doctors.

Minimum: Small flower.

Cloisterphobia: Fear of being caught in an elevator with a dozen nuns.

Born Loser: Someone who gets a paper-cut from a get well card.

Bacteria: The rear entrance to the cafeteria

Cabbage: The age of a taxi.

Doughnut: A boy who is crazy about money.

Campfire Conversations

Out of things to talk about? The following ticklers are great for making a campfire discussion livelier.

1. If you're in a vehicle going the speed of light, what happens when you turn the headlights on?
2. Why do they put braille dots on the keypad of the drive up ATM?
3. Is it Smoky Bear or Smoky the Bear?
4. Have you ever imagined a world without hypothetical questions?
5. If Pluto is Mickey Mouse's dog, what's Goofy?
6. When you have your picture taken with Mickey Mouse, does the guy inside the costume smile?
7. If Teflon is the worlds most non-stick surface, how do they get it to stick onto the pan?
8. What's the difference between a fat chance and a slim chance?
9. How many bouillon cubes can you make from one chicken?
10. How come Hawaii has interstate highways?
11. If 7-11 is open 24 hours a day, 365 days a year, how come there are locks on the door?
12. If you fill up your swimming pool with dry ice and melt it, can you swim in the pool without getting wet?
13. If you tied a piece of buttered toast to the back of a cat and dropped it from the top of the empire state building which would land facing up?
14. Do fish sleep?
15. Why do cockroaches turn over on their backs when they die? How do they turn over if they're dead?
16. Why isn't phonetics spelled the way it sounds?
17. Why do irons have a setting for permanent-press clothing?
18. What do they do with ice sculptures after they melt?
19. Why do they put an expiration date on sour cream? Isn't it already sour?
20. When sign makers go on strike, is anything painted on their signs?
21. How do you know when you've run out of invisible ink?
22. Where do camp rangers go to get away from it all?
23. What's the difference between a budding genius and a blooming idiot?
24. Why do they call them television sets when you only get one television?

25. Why is a package sent by land carrier called a shipment, while packages sent by sea are called cargo?

26. What do butterflies get in their stomachs when they're nervous?

27. Is a wedding successful if it comes off without a hitch?

28. Why do you call them apartments when they are attached to one another? Shouldn't they be called attachments?

29. Are people who jump off bridges in Paris in Siene?

30. Why are builders afraid to have a 13th floor, but publishers aren't afraid to have a chapter 11?

31. If quitters never win and winners never quit, how come you're supposed to quit while you are ahead?

32. When you open a box of cotton balls, do you need to throw out the one on top of the package?

33. When blondes have more fun, do they know it?

34. Why do television stations report power outages?

35. Do people go to Disney Land because of word of mouse advertising?

36. What hair color do they put on the driver's licenses of bald men?

37. What do you do if an endangered animal is eating an endangered plant?

38. What happens if you are scared half to death twice?

39. What does your nose smell like?

40. If the United States and Canada got into a war, where would the draft dodgers go?

41. What's the difference between an orange?

42. Is it shorter to New York or by train?

43. How tall is the empire state building? True or False?

44. Do you walk to school or do you carry your lunch?

45. Would you say a society of Atheists is a non-prophet organization?

46. Is there another word for synonym?

47. If you ate pasta and antipasto would you still be hungry?

48. Do you need a silencer if you are going to shoot a mime?

49. If pro is the opposite of con, is progress the opposite of congress?

50. What is another word for "thesaurus?"

51. If 75% of accidents occur within 5 miles of home, why not move 10 miles away?

52. If peanut butter cookies are made from peanut butter, then what are Girl Scout cookies made out of?

53. Is it warmer in the summer or in the country?

Campfire Introductions

It is the tradition that Scouting events are a "safe haven," for boys and for adult leaders; it is never proper for a campfire MC to use introductions to demean a Scout or an adult leader. Still, introductions are a great way to entertain during the lulls between campfire performances. The following humorous introductions when used properly with fellow camp staff members or with the permission of the individuals being introduced can add humor to your campfire and can turn the boring lulls into the most entertaining part of the evening.

Our next speaker has a fine voice, let's hope he doesn't ruin it by singing.

Our next singer reminds of a balloon, whenever he sings, I think I hear one leaking.

Our next singer sounds like a bird, and I'm sure you'll like this song if you enjoy the sound of a screech owl.

Our next storyteller is a second story man; no one ever believes his first story.

Our next speaker takes after the steeple that triggered Paul Revere's ride - he's a little light in the belfry.

Our next speaker thinks he's a real wit, and I have to tell you that I think he's half right.

I'm sure that many of you don't know that our next guest is an MD. That right, he's mentally deficient.

Our next speaker is very much like a vacation from school. That's right he's got no class

Our next song leader has a strong voice, strong enough to clean an oven.

I don't want to say our next song-leader is cheap but I hear he rides the outside horse on the merry-go-ride so that he can get a longer ride.

Our next singer loves cartoons; I understand he thinks a cartoon is a song you sing in the car.

Our next singer says he likes to read but I understand he thinks an autobiography is the life story of a car.

Our next speaker plans to become a bone specialist when he graduates from medical school. I think you'll agree he certainly has the head for it.

Our next speaker reminds me of a Scout knife, just one that is not very sharp.

We like to call our next singer chocolate bar. He's half nuts.

Everyone calls our next speaker Santa Claus because of all the old bags he hangs around with.

Our next singer is the kind of friend you can always depend on - he's always around when he needs you.

Our next speaker went to see a string quartet, and he was surprised to learn it wasn't four people playing tennis.

Our next song leader has a voice so husky it could pull a dog sled.

I like that last song. Some day you should put it to music.

Next time you should sing solo. So low no one can hear you.

Our last song leader couldn't carry a tune if it had a handle.

Our last singer needs to get a wheelbarrow - to carry his tunes in.

MC: What did you do with the money?
Speaker: What money?
MC: The money your parents gave you for voice lessons.

Scoutmaster's Minutes

It has long been a Scouting tradition to end campfires with a Scoutmaster's Minute. Scoutmaster's minutes are short stories with a moral that make a single point. They give Scouts something to think about as they return to their tents after a campfire. Some samples follow:

The Wisdom of Chief Sequassen

A Bird in the Hand

A young Indian brave was frustrated by Chief Sequassen. He thought the Chief was over the hill, and he wanted a new Chief. The young brave knew if he could make Chief Sequassen look like an "old fool" in front of the whole tribe, he would step down. But he also knew Chief Sequassen could be clever at times, so the brave would need a "fool proof" plan. The brave decided to get a small bird and hold it cupped in his hands. As he spoke, he would hold the bird saying, "Oh mighty Chief, in my hand I have an animal. You are wise beyond imagination. Please tell us what animal it is." If the Chief guessed wrong, the game would be over, as the mighty Chief had made a mistake. If he guessed right, the young brave would ask, "Is it alive or is it dead?" If the Chief said "dead", the brave would open his hand and the bird would fly away. If he said "alive", the brave would quickly close his hand on the bird and kill it; again proving the Chief less than all knowing.

The day came when the brave was to put his plan into action. When a lull came in the tribal council's conversation, the young brave jumped up. "Oh mighty Chief," he said, "I am holding a small animal. Can you tell me what it is?" Chief Sequassen said, "'While I am old the great spirit has given me great sight to see not only for the tribe, but to hunt well also. And I can see the tiniest feather from the tip of a finch, one of the smallest woodland creatures." The brave then said, "You are right, oh mighty Chief, but is it alive or is it dead?" The Chief grew thoughtful for a moment, and then he said, "The answer to that question, my young friend, is in your hands."

Faithful Deer

All the young Indians gathered around the campfire as Chief Sequassen recalled the story of Faithful Deer. When Faithful Deer was a young boy he became friends with Rugged Mountain. The two young Indians were inseparable, and they grew together in wisdom and in strength. The time came when the two were old enough to help provide for the needs of the tribe. So together they hunted wild turkey and game, in summer and winter, during blue sky and rain.

On one winter's day, Faithful Deer was overcome by sickness, so Rugged Mountain went out in search of food alone. Nighttime came and went, but Rugged Mountain did not return. The Chief called together all the people in the tribe and they began to search for Rugged Mountain. For three days Faithful Deer and the others searched in hilltops and valleys, on the plains and near the river, for their lost friend Rugged Mountain. And for three days, no sign of him was seen by anyone. A great storm settled over the area, and the Chief called his people together to stop the search for Rugged Mountain. "Our dear friend could not have survived this long in the wilderness alone," the Chief began. "A storm draws near and we must abandon our search for Rugged Mountain."

Faithful Deer was filled with grief. He could not give up hope that somewhere, somehow, Rugged Mountain was alive. So when nighttime fell he slipped away from the village and continued the search for his friend, alone. The falling snow made each step difficult, but Faithful Deer trudged on looking high and low for Rugged Mountain. After 3 more days had passed, Faithful Deer heard a cry in the distance. There, beyond the pine trees lay Rugged Mountain, badly injured and unable to walk.

"How did you manage to survive injured and alone, beaten by cold for all this time," Faithful Deer asked, as he embraced Rugged Mountain.

"I never doubted you would come my friend," Rugged Mountain replied. "The strength of our friendship kept me alive."

"So you see my children," Chief Sequassen concluded, "Loyalty carries with it the power of life over death."

A Scout is Loyal

The Dancing Brave

The young Indian brave wanted so much to be like the wise Chief Sequassen. He especially wanted to be able to dance like the old Chief did. While Chief Sequassen had lived many moons, everyone felt he was still the finest dancer in the tribe.

So the young brave went to the Chief and asked to be taught *all* of the dances. The Chief was very flattered, and seeing that the brave was sincere, he worked very closely with the brave for a whole year.

They both worked hard, and it came to pass that the brave was to perform some dances for the tribal council. After the dancing, the brave was disappointed with his performance. Although he had tried, the results just didn't satisfy him. So he sought out Chief Sequassen and asked him his opinion.

The Chief said, "I have taught you all the steps - and you have learned them well. Now you must hear the music yourself."

Leading the Horse

Chief Sequassen's tribe was spread across vast areas of the northeast, and once a year he would gather with the leaders of various tribal villages in order that they might all share their experiences. Included at one gathering was a younger leader who was having trouble convincing many of his braves to take a more active role in leading the tribe. He was frustrated and was having trouble justifying all his effort, and he was considering handing the tribal responsibilities over to someone else.

Chief Sequassen listened attentively and was sympathetic. He let the younger leader vent his frustrations. "You know," this young leader said, "I've shown them and shown them. I've taught them all the needed skills, but I can't seem to get any of these braves to step up and take the lead. I guess you can lead the horse to water but you can't make them drink."

Chief Sequassen offered a thoughtful reply, "Maybe you're job isn't to lead them. Perhaps your job is to make them thirsty so that they'll find the water themselves....."

The Quest for Knowledge

Twin brothers from a distant tribe reached the age in life where they leave the tribe on a quest for knowledge. The braves traveled in separate directions hoping to learn the ways of the world. Walking through the wilderness, the first brave stumbled upon Chief Sequassen.

"What are the people in your tribe like?" the first brave asked.

"Well," Chief Sequassen inquired, "How are the people in your tribe?"

"My tribe is filled with a bunch of miserable people who are always grumpy and unhappy," the first brave replied.

"You will find," the wise Chief responded, "that the people in this area are exactly the same way."

Later, the second brother also came upon the wise old Chief. "How are the people in your tribe," the second brave wondered.

"Well," Chief Sequassen inquired, "How are the people in your tribe?"

"Wonderful!" replied the other brother. "The people in our tribe are always cheerful and friendly, kind, loving and understanding."

"You will find," the wise Chief responded, "that the people in this area are exactly the same way." For you see the Chief understood, that the attitude of the people you meet, depends on your own state of mind. If you are happy and cheerful in everything you do, you will find the same in others.

A Scout is Cheerful

The Buffalo Stampede

A stampede of buffalo thundered across the plains in the direction of Chief Sequassen's tribe. When the tribes' people heard the sound of the approaching stampede, they began to run in a direction away from the approaching herd. Knowing his people could never outrun the herd; Chief Sequassen jumped on his horse and headed directly toward the head of the stampede.

When the buffalo saw the approaching Chief Sequassen, they shifted direction and traveled away from the settlement. Thankful tribes' people gathered around to praise the Chief for his courageous response. A young brave wondered about the Chief's action. "It all happened so fast," the brave observed. "How did you decide so quickly that riding into the herd was the best course of action to protect the tribe?"

"I did not think," the Chief replied. "I did not have to think. I have considered many times the possible danger a stampede would pose to the settlement, and I made up my mind many moons ago what I would do if this situation ever occurred. When it did, I acted instinctively."

A good Scout is prepared for all possibilities.

Putting Religion into Practice

There was a young brave who was struggling against a very stubborn illness. Chief Sequassen sent him to the medicine man who handed the brave some herbs that were certain to cure the ailment. The brave brought the herbs home and placed them next to his bed. The illness persisted. The illness progressed until the medicine man visited and told the boy to swallow the herbs. Within minutes, the ailment was cured.

The Indians believe that religion is like this medicine. If you don't ingest it, and make it a part of you, it has no value. You cannot simply belong to a religion. You must put it into practice.

A Scout is Reverent

The Ceremonial Headdress

A young brave and Chief Sequassen's daughter were in love and hoped to marry. So as was the tradition, the brave approached Chief Sequassen and asked what he could offer for the right to marry his daughter.

The Chief considered the question and then issued this reply, "My ceremonial headdress is quite old, and needs to be replaced. But it must be made by using only the finest materials, including berries from the Agwa bush, feathers from a bald eagle, thread from the Ickba tree, and shells from the great ocean. When the new headdress is complete, you may have my daughters hand in marriage."

So the brave sought out to gather materials for the headdress. But the Agwa bush was not yet in season, so Agwa berries would be hard to find. Shooting an eagle would be extremely difficult, and finding one of the few very rare Ickba trees would also be a great challenge. Finally, the great ocean was far away, and it would take great effort to recover the shells.

So the brave decided to take a few shortcuts in preparing the headdress. He found berries from the Caca bush which he used in place of Agwa berries. He used the feathers from a hawk, thread from the Nebee tree, and freshwater shells from a nearby lake. When the headdress was done he presented it to Chief Sequassen for his approval. The Chief was very pleased. "I can see you worked hard to prepare this headdress," the Chief began. "Such materials are difficult to collect and you deserve praise for uncovering them so quickly. I am sorry to say, however, that the Chief from a neighboring tribe has presented me with a new ceremonial headdress as a symbol of peace and friendship. I feel compelled to use that headdress now, so I would like you to have the one that you prepared as a wedding gift from me. This beautiful headdress is a picture of your own character, true and loyal from top to bottom."

Imagine how the young brave must have felt! The ceremonial headdress was indeed a picture of his character, and during his wedding ceremony, and throughout his life, when he placed it on his head he would be reminded of his dishonesty, and the shallowness of his character.

A Scout is trustworthy

Too-ka'

Chief Sequassen took the young Indian braves on a trip, to help prepare them to become warriors. Among the braves was a boy named Too-ka'. Too-ka' believed that he was the finest young Indian born since the mighty Chief. Above all he wanted everyone, especially Chief Sequassen, to be impressed with his wilderness skills.

But things did not go well for Too-ka', as he was paired with a group of braves who burned their supper. "You have ruined our food," Too-ka' complained to the others. Too-ka' next began a small carving project, which ended when he was cut with his own knife. "You bumped me," Too-ka wined, as he bandaged his hand. Finally, when night set in, the young braves retired to shelters that they had constructed. A strong wind blew, and the shelter Too-ka' was sharing collapsed. "You idiots," Too-ka' yelled, "You didn't construct the lean-to properly."

The next day Too-ka' approached the Chief and asked, "Why am I constantly affected by the foolishness of others."

"When bad things happen to us," the Chief explained, "the first place to look for the cause is within ourselves."

Giving

It was a long standing custom that when the Chief of the tribe entered old age he would divide his horses among three promising braves. Tradition allowed Chief Sequassen to keep his best horse, but the remainder should be divided with half going to the top brave, one third to the second brave and one ninth to the final brave. Unfortunately, Chief Sequassen would have only 17 horses remaining if he kept one for himself. So, in spite of his great affection for his best horse, he decided to add his favorite to the group making 18, a number that could easily be divided. Then he gave 9 horses to his top brave, six to a second brave and two to the last. One horse remained, the one that the Chief loved best, and he took it back for himself.

The Indians like to say that when you give away that which you love, it will be returned to you.

Faithful Deer

All the young Indians gathered around the campfire as Chief Sequassen recalled the story of the Faithful Deer. When Faithful Deer was a young boy he became friends with Rugged Mountain. The two young Indians were inseparable, and they grew together in wisdom and strength. The time came when the two were old enough to help provide for the needs of the tribe. So together they hunted wild turkey and game, in summer and winter, during blue sky and rain.

On one winter's day, Faithful Deer was overcome by sickness, so Rugged Mountain went out in search of food alone. Nighttime came and went, but Rugged Mountain did not return. The Chief called together all the people in the tribe and they began to search for Rugged Mountain. So when nighttime fell he slipped away from the village and continued the search for his friend, alone. The falling snow made each step difficult, but Faithful Deer trudged on looking high and low for Rugged Mountain. After 3 more days had passed, Faithful Deer heard a cry in the distance. There, beyond the pine trees lay Rugged Mountain, badly injured and unable to walk.

"How did you manage to survive injures and alone, beaten by cold for all this time," Faithful Deer asked as he embraced Rugged Mountain.
"I never doubted you would come my friend," Rugged Mountain replied. "The Strength of our friendship kept me alive."

"So you see my children," Chief Sequassen concluded, "Loyalty carries with it the power of life over death.

A Scout is loyal

Scary Stories with a Humorous Twist

An Encounter with the Moon Lake Monster

Back in 1948 a veteran from the Second World War decided to spend a quiet day fishing on Moon Lake in Vickers Heights, Ontario. The man had seen a lot during the war and it had caused him to loose his faith in humanity and his faith in God. Without warning the veteran's boat was attacked by the Moon Lake Monster. In one easy flip, the beast tossed the man out of his boat and high into the air. Then it opened its mouth making ready to swallow the surprised soldier. As the man sailed head over heels, he cried out, "Oh, God. Help me!"

At once, the ferocious attack scene froze in place, and as the unbeliever hung in mid-air, a booming voice came down from the clouds, "I thought you didn't believe in me?"

"Come on God, give me a break!!" the man pleaded. "Two minutes ago I didn't believe in the Moon Lake monster either!"

An Encounter with a Bear

In the late 1960's a man came to this area to hunt for bears. At the time there was still a large bear population in this area. As he trudged through the forest looking for the beasts, he came upon a large and steep hill. Thinking that perhaps there might be a bear on the other side of the hill, the man climbed the steep incline. Just as he was pulling himself up over the last outcropping of rocks, a huge bear met him nose to nose.

The bear roared fiercely and the man was so scared that he lost his balance and began rolling down the hill with the bear pursuing him as he went. In the process of falling down the hill, the man lost his gun. When he finally stopped rolling near the bottom of the hill he discovered that he had broken his leg. Escape was impossible, and so the man, who had never been particularly religious prayed, "God, if you will make this bear a Christian I will be happy with whatever lot you give me for the rest of my life."

The bear was no more than three feet away from the man when it stopped dead in its tracks... looked up to the heavens quizzically... and then fell to its knees and began to pray, "O Lord, bless this food of which I am about to receive from thy bounty........"

Ghost Stories

Army of the Dead

A taxi driver moved his family from New York to Charleston 10 years after the close of the Civil War. The driver had found a job on the late shift and each night he left his wife and son to make the evening rounds. The boy of 13 was having trouble adjusting to his new environment. Each night after he had fallen a sleep he was awakened at the stroke of midnight by the rumble of heavy wheels passing in the street in front of his house. His family lived on a dead end street, and there was no explanation for the noise. Each night when the boy awoke he wandered toward the front of the house to see what caused the commotion. But each night his mother stopped him, forbidding him to look out the front window to investigate the sound.

One day at school, he asked a boy in the neighborhood what was the cause of the nightly sound. The neighbor boy said, "What you are hearing is the Army of the Dead. They are Confederate soldiers who died in a nearby hospital without knowing that the war was over. Each night, they rise from their graves in search of Yankee soldiers."

The following night the young boy pretended to fall asleep. Away from his mother's watchful eye, he climbed out the back window and walked to the front of the house so he could see the Army of the Dead walk past. Before midnight a thick fog rolled in. Within the fog he could see the shapes of horses and hear gruff human voices. He heard the rumble of heavy cannons being dragged through the street, followed by the thunder of hundreds of feet marching in cadence. For what seemed like an eternity hundreds of soldiers shrouded in gray passed before his eyes. Then off in the distance was the sound of a bugle blast and the words charge. A single shot rang out, followed by an eerie silence.

In a daze the boy took his first step to walk back toward his home when he felt a sharp pain in his thigh. He glanced down to see blood spurting from his upper leg. In a stupor he dragged himself to the nearby hospital that had treated so many confederate soldiers years before. No one has been able to explain how a lone confederate bullet made its way into a young boy's leg 10 years after the end of the civil war. The boy now walks with a heavy limp, a lifetime mark on a boy who dared to look at the Army of the Dead.

The Devil in the Mississippi

They say that the devil was in the Mississippi River; you could feel it with every spurt of water that splashed against the boats. You could hear it in the jangle of every bell, feel it in every eddy that swirled, and see it in the dim light of lanterns that tried to pierce the dense fog. You could hear it in the chug of every engine. There was no doubt that the devil was in the Mississippi River, and no captain dared take his ship out on that fateful night.

No captain, that is, except for Willie McGee. It was a bad night to be out in a paddleboat, but Willie had sworn when he set out that nothing could make him turn back. The other captains were huddled in the tavern, speaking ill and offering empty boasts. After listening to these boasts for hours, Willie made one himself. He knew the Mississippi River so well that he could guide his paddleboat on his run even through the thickness of this foggy night. The other pilots laughed and told Willie he would return before midnight. But Willie grew angry at their jeers and he vowed that he would not turn back, even if the devil should bar his way!

The river's current grew uncharacteristically swift as Willie approached the bend near Vicksburg. The paddle wheeler spun oddly under the swirling eddies of the gushing river. But Willie knew every turn and guided the boat along despite the thick fog. He was almost to Vicksburg when he saw shore where no shore had ever been before. How could this be? He had piloted his paddleboat through this area dozens of times before. How could there be shore directly in front of him?

The only explanation could be that the mighty Mississippi had shifted its course! It seems Satan must have heard Willie's challenge at the tavern that night. Willie swore every curse he knew, while relentlessly searching for a way through. He had sworn he would complete his run without turning back and he was going to find a way to make it. There was no turning back! He would stay on the river until sunrise if he had to!

Without warning, the paddleboat lurched violently. The engine sputtered and stalled. The boat began to list as water breached its bow. The next day the fog finally lifted, but not before Willie McGee and his paddleboat sank to the bottom of the mighty Mississippi. Locals say that on foggy nights you can still hear the ring of the bell, the sound of the engine and the curses of the ghost captain, Willie McGee, trying to complete his run.

Order your Scout Fun Books today!

Scout Riddles

Superior Campfires

The Scout Puzzle & Activity Book

Scout Skits

Scout Jokes

Scoutmaster's Minutes

Scoutmaster's Minutes II

More Scout Skits

Along the Scouting Trail

Campfire Tales

Run-ons and Even More Scout Skits

Scout Games

For an updated list of available books along with current pricing visit: *scoutfunbooks.webs.com*
or find our books on Amazon!

Books are also available on a wholesale basis to qualified Scout Troops, Council Shops, trading posts in quantities of 50 or more. Contact us by email at BoyScoutBooks@aol.com.

Printed in Great Britain
by Amazon.co.uk, Ltd.,
Marston Gate.